THE POCKET
CUBISM

Published in 2025
by Gemini Gift Books
Part of Gemini Books Group

Based in Woodbridge and London

Marine House, Tide Mill Way,
Woodbridge, Suffolk IP12 1AP
United Kingdom

www.geminibooks.com

Text and Design © 2025 Gemini Gift Books Ltd
Part of the Gemini Pockets series

Cover illustration by Natalie Foss
Text by Roland Hall

ISBN 978-1-80247-327-8

A CIP catalogue record for this book is available from the British Library.

Manufacturer's EU Representative: Eurolink Compliance Limited, 25 Herbert Place,
Dublin, D02 AY86, Republic of Ireland. admin@eurolink-europe.ie

Printed in China

10 9 8 7 6 5 4 3 2 1

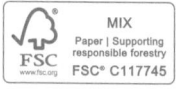

MIX
Paper | Supporting
responsible forestry
FSC® C117745
www.fsc.org

Picture credits: Alamy Stock Photo: Stefano Politi Markovina 4; Lebrecht Music
& Arts 20; Aclosund Historic 30; Science History Images 42, 52; The Print Collector
68; The History Collection 78; GRANGER - Historical Picture Archive 90; Tim Wright
108. Getty Images: Choumoff 98; ullstein bild Dtl. 116. Shutterstock: Mister-john 8;
Ardkyuu 92-97; Lucie Batkova 10-11; Bibadash 80-89; Anastasiia Hevko 70-77; JAY404
54-66; Lepusinensis 100-107; Sylfida 110-113; TWINS DESIGN STUDIO 118-128).

THE
POCKET

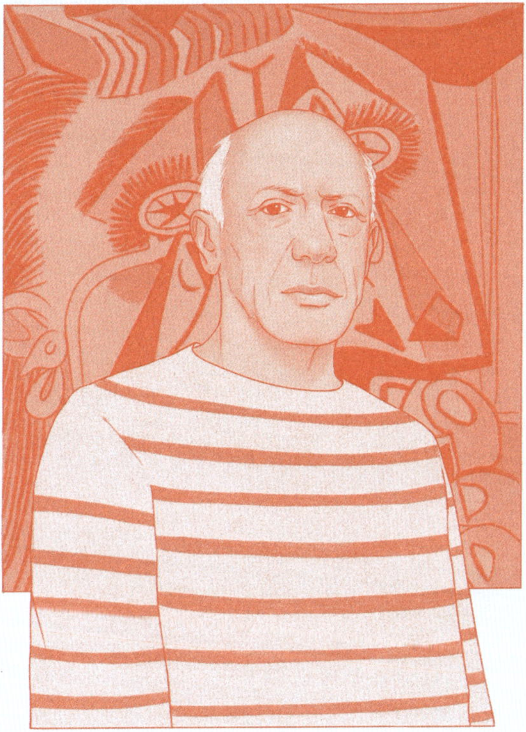

CUBISM

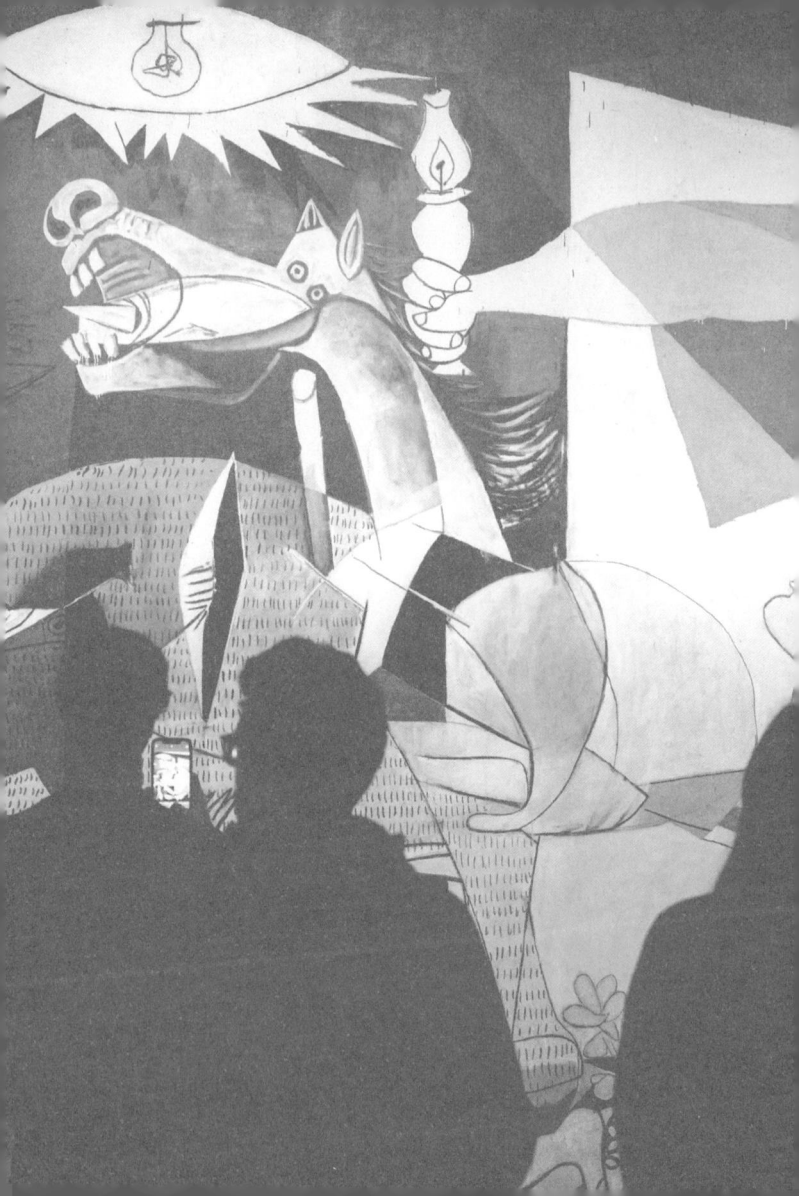

CONTENTS

INTRODUCTION

Cubism is an early twentieth-century art movement that developed in Paris and swiftly revolutionized both painting and sculpture globally.

Cubist artists divided objects into geometric shapes, showing multiple perspectives at once, instead of aiming for a realistic representation of subject matter.

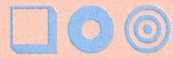

Cubism focused on structure, form and abstraction. This challenged traditional ideas of space and depth in art.

It was pioneered by Pablo Picasso and Georges Braque in Paris, and the movement went on to influence art, architecture and design. It reshaped the way we understand and portray visual reality. Cubism remains a cornerstone of modernist art.

ORIGINS & INFLUENCES

WHAT IS CUBISM?

Cubism was a modern art movement that depicted its subjects from multiple viewpoints simultaneously ("faceting of form"). The artists divided their paintings into geometric shapes that gave a more conceptual portrayal of a subject rather than a realistic reproduction. The art form challenged traditional perspectives through its emphasis on abstraction.

Cubism was revolutionary in that it challenged the fundamental nature of how art was represented and viewed, in terms of space, form and structure.

ORIGINS

Cubism originated in Paris in the early 1900s. At the time, artists wanted to move beyond realistic portrayals of their subjects, for example, through Impressionism and Expressionism.

Another influence was African and Iberian art, particularly the abstract forms and geometric shapes seen in tribal masks.

Crucially, Paul Cézanne (1838–1906) was using geometric simplification in his work, although he died before the Cubist movement was formally established.

EARLY WORKS

In 1904 and 1907, two exhibitions of Cézanne's paintings were displayed in Paris. Some of his work had an almost three-dimensional form, portraying the subject from more than one angle and using geometric shapes.

This influenced various painters, particularly the Spanish artist Pablo Picasso (1881-1973), who was experimenting with new ways to represent three-dimensional forms on canvas. His painting *The Ladies of Avignon* marked a turning point.

In 1912 in Barcelona, the first Cubist group exhibition was held. It featured work by Jean Metzinger, Albert Gleizes and Juan Gris.

THE LADIES OF AVIGNON

BY PABLO PICASSO, 1907

Location: Museum of Modern Art, New York, USA

This work was highly controversial when first painted and viewed, although it was not publicly exhibited until 1916, when Cubism was well established. The women in the painting are viewed from different perspectives, giving a fractured representation that was completely different from other artwork at that time.

HOUSES AT L'ESTAQUE

BY GEORGES BRAQUE, 1908

Location: Lille Métropole Museum of Modern, Contemporary and Outsider Art, Lille, France

When Braque submitted this painting to the Salon des Beaux-Arts in Paris, it was met with derision, and Henri Matisse described it as a painting made up of little cubes. From that, the Cubist movement gained its name. The painting is significant for that very reason: separate, geometric elements make up a whole.

EVOLUTION

Cubism evolved in two main phases. The first was Analytical Cubism (*c.* 1907–12), when the artists broke objects into angular fragments and used muted colour palettes.

Later, Synthetic Cubism (*c.* 1912–19) introduced brighter colours, simpler shapes and elements of collage.

Cubism spread across Europe, influencing other styles, such as Futurism and Constructivism, and laying the groundwork for modern abstract and conceptual art.

ARTISTS

Pablo Picasso and Georges Braque
were the founders of Cubism.

Subsequently, Juan Gris, Fernand
Léger and Robert Delaunay expanded
the style. Each artist had a slightly
different approach: Gris with precise
compositions, Léger with mechanized,
robotic forms and Delaunay with
more vibrant colour.

VIOLIN AND CANDLESTICK

BY GEORGES BRAQUE, 1910

Location: San Francisco Museum of Modern Art, California, USA

An example of Analytical Cubism, this is a dynamic and energetic painting, despite its sombre colour palette. A still life, it clearly demonstrates Braque's innovative approach with which he represented three-dimensional objects on flat canvas, as they are broken into geometric forms that explore multiple perspectives at the same time.

STYLE

Cubist style features fragmented forms, overlapping planes and multiple perspectives within a single work of art.

The artists used geometric shapes and muted, or limited, colour palettes, especially in the early days of the movement.

Later works include brighter colours and collage. Cubist artists invited the viewer to reinterpret their perception and understanding of space, depth and subject matter.

INFLUENCES

Cubism was the starting point for subsequent art movements, including Surrealism, Art Deco, Dada and Futurism. It also influenced Pop Art, with its bright colours, shapes and use of varied media.

The movement also prompted innovation in music, with fragmented melodies, for example, in the work of Igor Stravinsky (1882–1971) and Erik Satie (1866–1925). It also influenced literature; Gertrude Stein's unconventional poems in *Tender Buttons* (1914) and James Joyce's *Ulysses* (1922) are good examples.

Architect Le Corbusier (1887–1965) was inspired by Cubism's structural ideas; a significant example is the geometric abstraction of Villa La Roche, Paris, France.

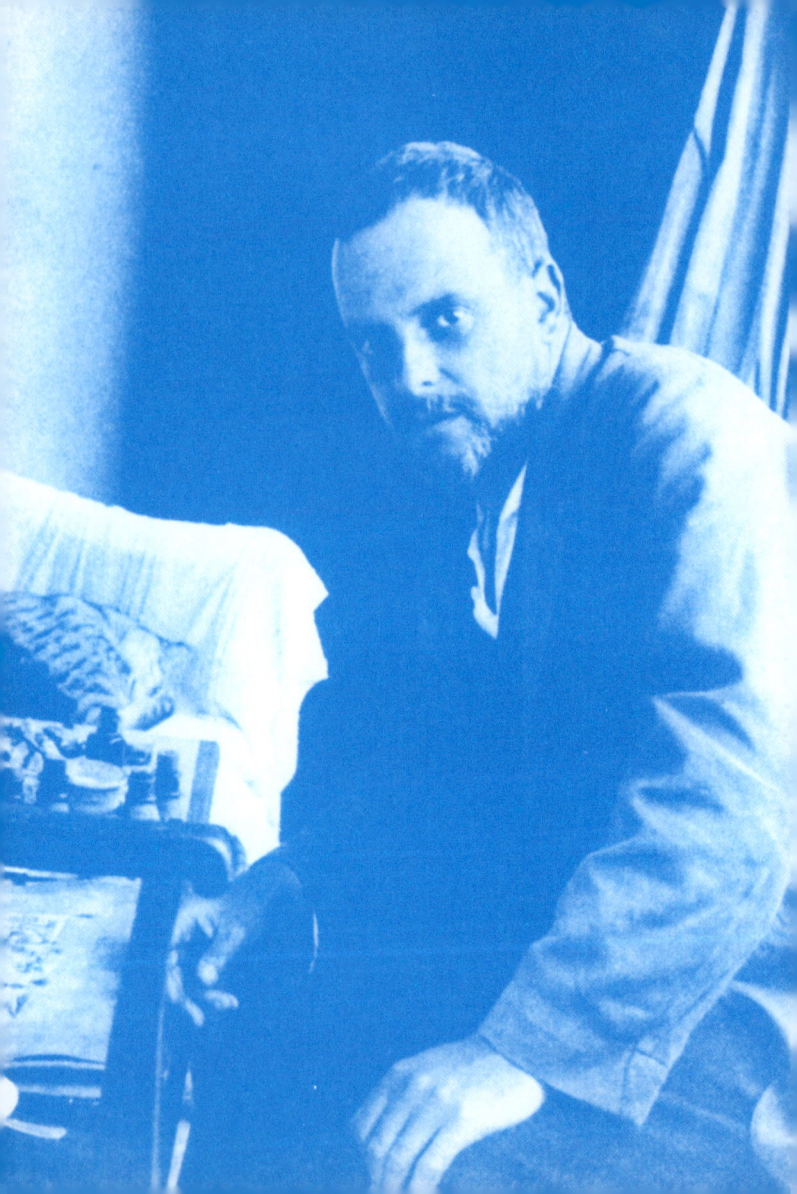

PAUL KLEE

1879–1940

Place of birth/death:

Munchenbuchsee, Switzerland/
Locarno, Switzerland

Key works:

Hammamet with Its Mosque (1914)
Villa R (1919)
Miraculous Landing, or the "112!" (1920)
The Twittering Machine (1922)
Highway and Byways (1928)

EARLY YEARS

Paul Klee was born in Switzerland to a German father, who was a music teacher, and a Swiss mother, who was a singer. He was encouraged to pursue a career in music, and at a young age it was clear he was a very talented violinist, as well as a keen illustrator. In 1898, contrary to his parents' wishes and expectations, Klee studied art at Munich's Academy of Fine Arts.

"The conviction
that painting is the
right profession
grows stronger
and stronger in me.
Writing is the only
other thing I still feel
attracted to. Perhaps
when I am mature
I shall go back to it."

PAUL KLEE,
THE DIARIES OF PAUL KLEE, 1964

"Trees are violated, humans become incapable of life; there is a coercion that leads to the unrecognizability of the object, to a picture-puzzle!"

PAUL KLEE,
KANDINSKY AND KLEE IN TUNISIA BY ROGER
BENJAMIN WITH CRISTINA ASHJIAN, 2015

HAMMAMET WITH ITS MOSQUE

BY PAUL KLEE, 1914

Location: Berggruen Klee Collection, New York, USA

Hammamet with Its Mosque is a watercolour, and an exercise by the artist in contrast and colour. It features both representational and non-representational elements and combines the abstract geometry of Cubism with elements of Islamic architecture. This creates a striking blend of structure and emotion.

STYLE

Klee has been associated with multiple art movements, including Expressionism, Cubism and Abstraction. Although not solely a Cubist artist, Klee incorporated many of the elements of the movement, particularly in his paintings around 1912–15, and Cubist elements can still be seen in Klee's work from his Bauhaus years. A good example is in the ink, pencil and watercolour work from 1922, *Affected Place*, with its limited colours and geometric objects.

BAUHAUS

The Bauhaus was a revolutionary German art and design school founded in 1919 by Walter Gropius (1883–1969). It aimed to unify art, craft and technology, with an emphasis on minimalist, functional design.

Klee was a key figure, teaching there from 1921 to 1931. He brought a poetic approach to the school's theories of design and structure. Klee's work and teaching blended colour theory, abstraction and symbolism, helping to shape the Bauhaus's mixture of art, craft and modernity.

LATER YEARS

Klee's later works became increasingly abstract and surreal, until he died in 1940 at the age of 60.

The artist's influence on many subsequent painters, illustrators and printmakers is evident, with his bold colours, strong lines, and fascinating signs and symbols. His colour work during the Bauhaus years has been hugely influential, too.

"Colour has taken possession of me; no longer do I have to chase after it, I know that it has hold of me forever... Colour and I are one. I am a painter."

PAUL KLEE,
A CONCISE HISTORY OF MODERN PAINTING
BY HERBERT READ, 1968

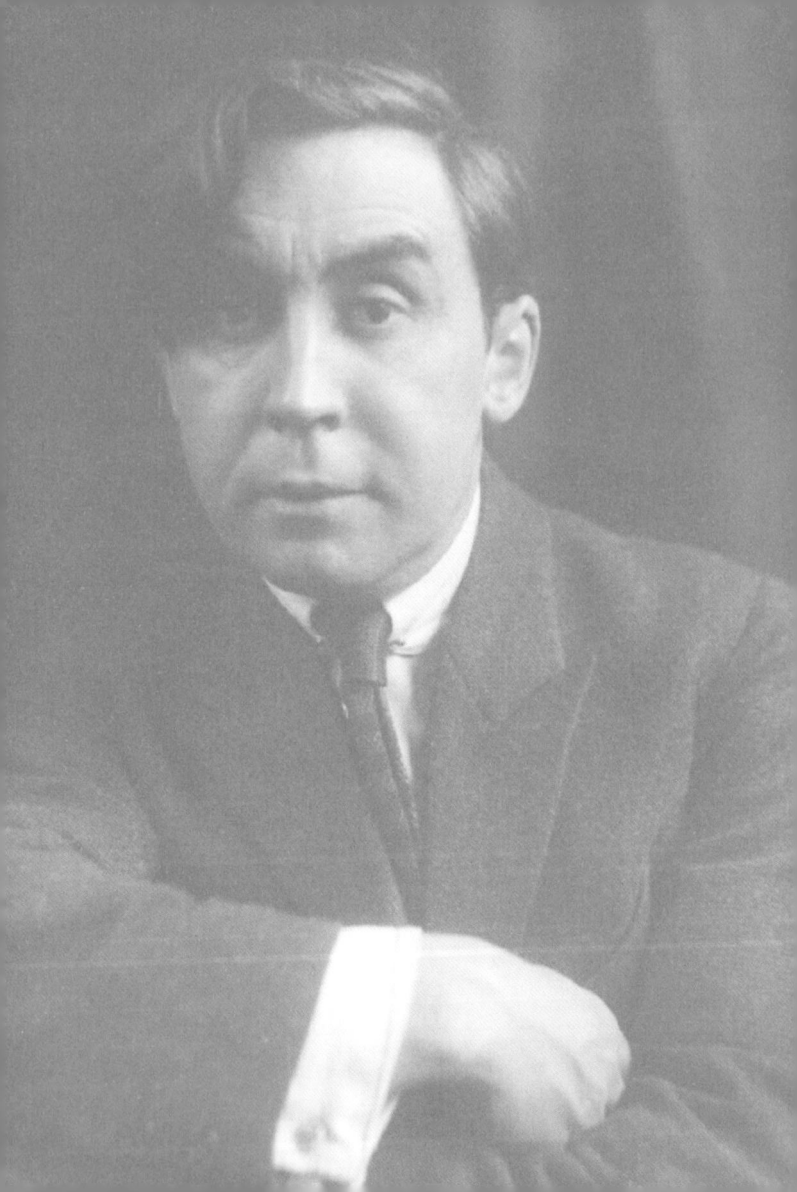

ALBERT GLEIZES

1881–1953

Place of birth/death:

Paris, France/ Saint-Rémy-de-Provence, France

Key works:

Countryside (1902)
Woman with Phlox (1910)
The Bathers (1912)
Composition for "Jazz" (1915)
Woman with Black Glove (1920)

EARLY YEARS

Albert Léon Gleizes was born in 1881 in Paris, where his father was a fabric designer. After he left school, Gleizes joined the army and then decided to pursue a career as a painter.

Early inspiration for his work came from the Impressionists, notably Alfred Sisley and Camille Pissarro, and the influence of the two painters can be seen in Gleizes' early landscape works.

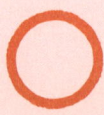

"We wish to dazzle others with that which we daily snatch from the world of sense."

ALBERT GLEIZES,
"CUBISM" BY ALBERT GLEIZES AND JEAN
METZINGER, 1913

INSPIRATION

Gleizes enjoyed early success as an artist, and by 1908 he displayed some pieces in an exhibition in Moscow.

His work evolved, and with influence from Fauvism, his paintings began to resemble those of the Cubist artists in Paris: people were broken down into distinct shapes and colours, with multiple facets.

Gleizes became an important part of the Cubist movement and his work was part of the first Cubist exhibition, which took place in Paris in 1911.

DIFFERENT CUBES

Gleizes had a different outlook from the "core" Cubists such as Picasso and Braque. He tended not to paint still lifes, preferring larger pieces that looked at the wider world with more significant cultural or societal meaning, including sporting events and other, larger groups of people.

Gleizes did not paint in an Analytical Cubist fashion, and became more of an abstract painter as his personal style developed.

"At this moment Cubism is painting."

ALBERT GLEIZES,
"CUBISM" BY ALBERT GLEIZES
AND JEAN METZINGER, 1913

"CUBISM"

Albert Gleizes and Jean Metzinger wrote the book *"Cubism"* together. It was first published in 1912.

Here, they defined Cubism as a pursuit of higher, structural truths beyond realism. The book emphasizes multiple perspectives, intellectual order and autonomy in art. In doing so, it effectively laid out a philosophical foundation for modern abstract painting.

CONTROVERSY

After a Cubist exhibition in Paris in 1912, questions were asked in the French parliament regarding the use of public funds to support art that was viewed by many people as "barbaric".

Shortly afterwards, in 1913, Gleizes travelled to the USA and exhibited at the Armory Show in New York. It was one of the first Cubist exhibitions outside France.

"I wish to establish the true history of Cubism whose beginning was not a matter of mere chance."

ALBERT GLEIZES,
THE EPIC, FROM IMMOBILE FORM TO MOBILE FORM, 1925

LATER LIFE

After the First World War, Gleizes became more religious, and this affected the style and content of his work. His painting became more abstract, with an emphasis on geometry, and reflected ideas from Medieval Christian art and theology.

He continued to paint and write, penning various important works about spirituality and art.

In his book *La Forme et l'Histoire* (1932) he connected geometry to Christian metaphysics, placing an emphasis on unity and cosmic order.

"A terrible thing has happened to me: I believe I am finding God."

ALBERT GLEIZES,
ALBERT GLEIZES 1881–1953,
A RETROSPECTIVE EXHIBITION,
NEW YORK, 1953

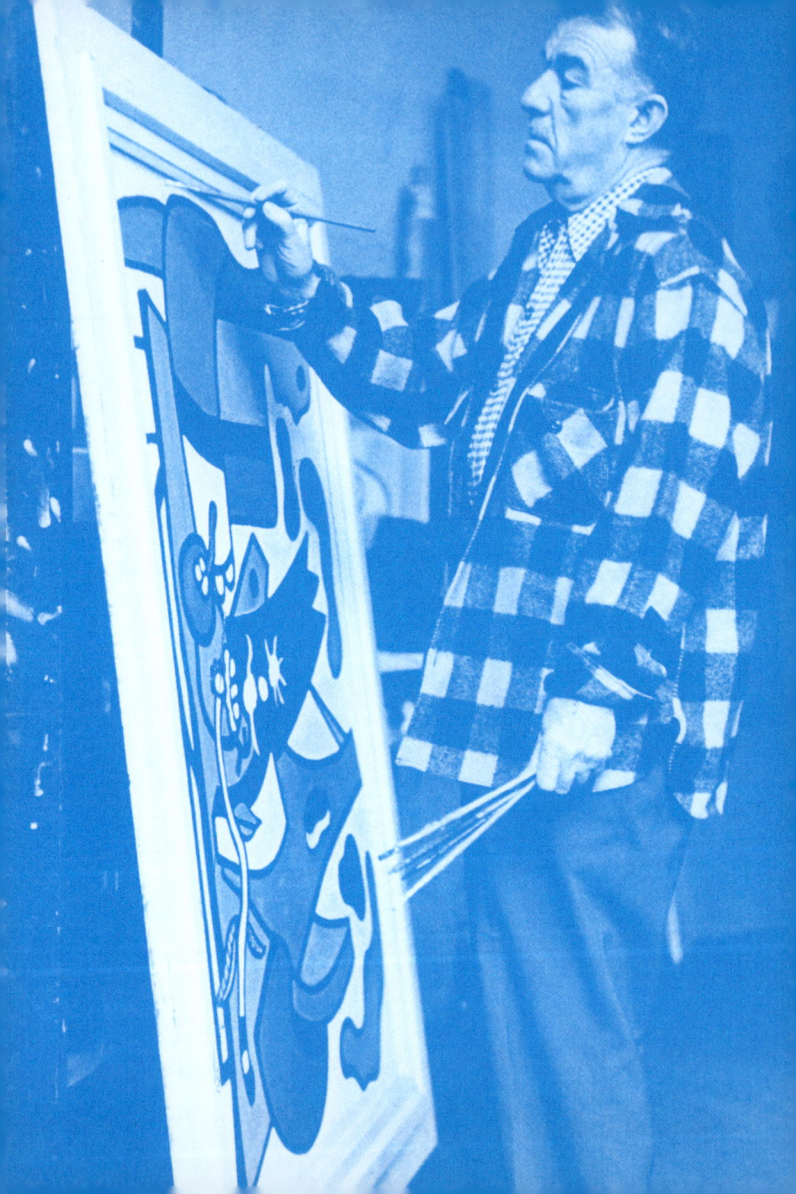

FERNAND LÉGER

1881–1955

Place of birth/death:

Argentan, France/Gif-sur-Yvette, France

Key works:

Nudes in the Forest (1910)
Contrast of Forms (1913)
The Card Players (1917)
Mona Lisa with Keys (1930)
The Big Black Divers (1944)

EARLY YEARS

Joseph Fernand Henri Léger was born in Normandy, France in 1881. His father was a cattle dealer, but Léger initially undertook training in an architect's office in Caen. After his obligatory military service, he moved to Paris to study at the École des Arts Décoratifs and Académie Julian.

Léger worked as an architectural illustrator during this time, and he attended the 1907 Paul Cézanne retrospective exhibition in Paris, which was to influence his work.

CUBISM CALLING

Léger's work until 1907 showed an influence from the Impressionists, but that changed in 1911 when he exhibited *Nudes in the Forest* (1910) in Paris. It was Cubist in content and style.

Another example of his early Cubist work is *The Fruit Bowl on the Table* (1909), which is reminiscent of the work of fellow artists Pablo Picasso and Georges Braque.

WAR

Léger's career as an artist was cut short by the First World War when he was drafted in 1914. He fought in the Battle of Verdun in 1916, where he suffered the effects of gas and was sent home. His painting *Soldiers Playing Cards* (1917) features robot-like figures.

The experience of battle had a profound effect on Léger's work. After the war he took more interest in the human figure and his work became less abstract.

TUBISM

Léger's work evolved from Cubism to a bolder, more mechanized aesthetic style. He was initially influenced by Picasso and Braque and their sombre tones. After 1919 he embraced bright colours, tubular forms and industrial themes. His work became more graphic and accessible.

The term "tubism" was used to describe his work, which featured cylinders and robot-like characters.

VARIETY

During the 1920s, Léger was prolific in many forms of creative expression. As well as painting, he drew illustrations for books, the most famous of which is *The End of the World Filmed by the Angel of Notre Dame* (1929). It is a landmark of modernist book design and demonstrated Léger's "machine aesthetic", the style characterized by his fascination with and depiction of the modern, industrial world.

NUDES IN THE FOREST

BY FERNAND LÉGER, 1910

Location: Kröller-Muller State Museum, Otterlo, Netherlands

This was Léger's first major work that follows the Cubist style. *Nudes in the Forest* clearly demonstrates the elements that define the artist's own personal form of Cubism, including his use of a distinct monochromatic colour pallet and his unique geometric style that was more industrial than other Cubists.

"I myself have employed the close-up, which is the cinema's only real invention."

FERNAND LÉGER,
FERNAND LÉGER – THE LATER YEARS, 1988

LATER YEARS

During the Second World War Léger moved to the USA, where he worked with artists in New York and lectured at Yale University. He returned to France in 1945 and continued to work until his death in 1955, often on large-scale artworks, including murals and stained-glass windows.

Léger's influence is significant. His vibrant colour use and abstract style was very popular with modern American artists, and he was a key influence on the Pop Art movement.

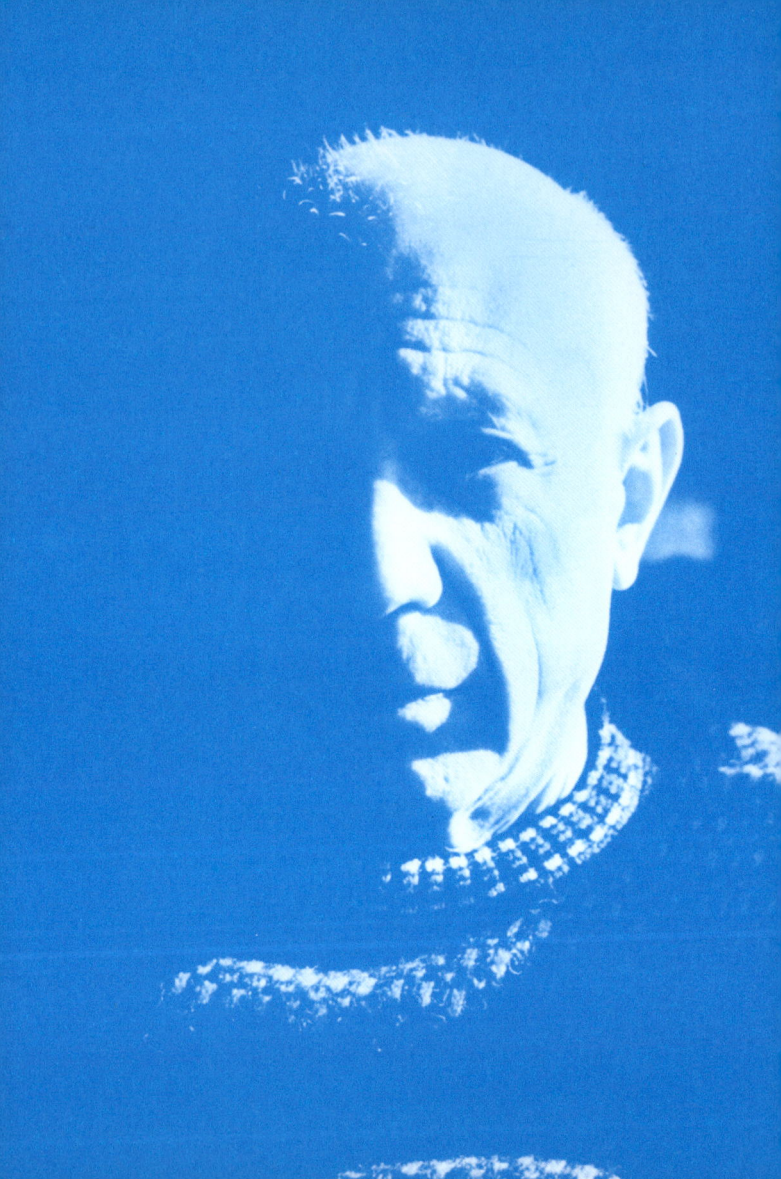

PABLO PICASSO

1881–1973

Place of birth/death:

Málaga Spain/Mougins, France

Key works:

The Ladies of Avignon (1907)
Ma Jolie (1911–12)
Bowl of Fruit, Violin and Bottle (1914)
The Three Musicians (1921)
Guernica (1937)

EARLY YEARS

The birth name of the artist we know as Pablo Picasso was Pablo Diego José Francisco de Paula Juan Nepomuceno María de los Remedios Cipriano de la Santísima Trinidad Ruiz y Picasso.

He was born in 1881 in Málaga in Spain, where his father was an art professor. The young Picasso showed exceptional artistic talent from an early age.

CONTENT

Picasso explored a wide range of subjects throughout his extensive career: portraits, nudes, still lifes, mythology, war and love. He frequently returned to the female form, bullfighting and the figure of the artist in his paintings. Some of his works reflects personal experiences – he painted many portraits of his lovers – and even political events, such as *Guernica* (1937).

PARIS

Picasso moved to Paris, the centre of the European art scene, in 1900. He lived in abject poverty, sharing an apartment with the poet Max Jacob.

Picasso immersed himself in avant-garde circles and absorbed many different artistic influences, including Post-Impressionism, Symbolism, Fauvism and African and Iberian art.

He took particular interest in Vincent Van Gogh's expressive brushwork and, as other Cubists, Cézanne's reduction of nature to geometric shapes.

BOWL OF FRUIT, VIOLIN AND BOTTLE

BY PABLO PICASSO, 1912

Location: Philadelphia Museum of Art, Pennsylvania, USA

This painting exemplifies Synthetic Cubism, as familiar objects are fragmented and reassembled into a dynamic composition of overlapping planes and textures. The muted colour palette and abstract forms challenge traditional representations, and invite the viewer to decipher the still life in front of them.

"Painting is a blind man's profession. He paints not what he sees, but what he feels, what he tells himself about what he has seen."

PABLO PICASSO,
THE JOURNALS OF JEAN COCTEAU, 1956

STYLE

Around 1907, Picasso, alongside Georges Braque, pioneered Cubism. Among other styles, the two were inspired by the simplified forms of non-Western art, and they began to visually dismantle and reassemble objects from multiple viewpoints. This revolutionary approach was first seen in works such as *The Ladies of Avignon* (1907), which shattered traditional notions of perspective and marked a radical departure from Western art.

"My work is a
constructive one.
I am building,
not tearing
down."

PABLO PICASSO
THE ATLANTIC, 1957

EVOLUTION

Picasso's early phase of Cubism involved the breaking down of subjects into fragmented geometric shapes and presenting them on a flattened picture plane. Colour was often muted in an attempt to emphasize form and structure of the subject. Picasso's early Cubist works challenged viewers to piece together the depicted object themselves, engaging with a new visual language.

SYNTHETIC CUBISM

From about 1912, Picasso and Braque evolved Cubism into its Synthetic phase. This involved building up compositions using simpler, more symbolic shapes and introducing collage elements such as newspaper and wallpaper. They used colour more extensively, and their focus shifted towards constructing new realities rather than simply dissecting existing ones.

GUERNICA

BY PABLO PICASSO, 1937

Location: Museo Reina Sofía, Madrid, Spain

Picasso's response to the bombing of a Basque town during the Spanish Civil War was this huge painting. In stark black, white and grey, it depicts twisted people and animals in disarray, capturing the suffering of the innocent and the horror of war without graphic realism. It is an emotionally powerful and symbolically rich painting, and a significant anti-war piece (see page 4).

PROLIFIC

Over a career that spanned roughly 75 years, Picasso's artistic output totalled 14,000 paintings and drawings, 100,000 prints, 24,000 book illustrations, and 300 models and sculptures.

POST-CUBISM

Picasso's relentless experimentation pushed the boundaries of Cubism. He explored different facets of the style, from portraiture to still life, constantly innovating and influencing other artists, including those outside the movement.

Picasso's ability to combine diverse influences and his unwavering commitment to pushing artistic conventions cemented his central role in the Cubist movement.

FINAL YEARS

Even in his later years, Picasso
was incredibly prolific and
creatively restless. He continued
to experiment with painting,
sculpture and printmaking,
and he often revisited earlier
themes and styles with a fresh
perspective. He lived in the
south of France and enjoyed
immense fame, working until
his death in 1973 at the age of 91.
He left behind an enormous and
influential body of work.

"Nature and art, being two different things, cannot be the same thing."

PABLO PICASSO,
FUTURISM BY DIDIER OTTINGER, 2008

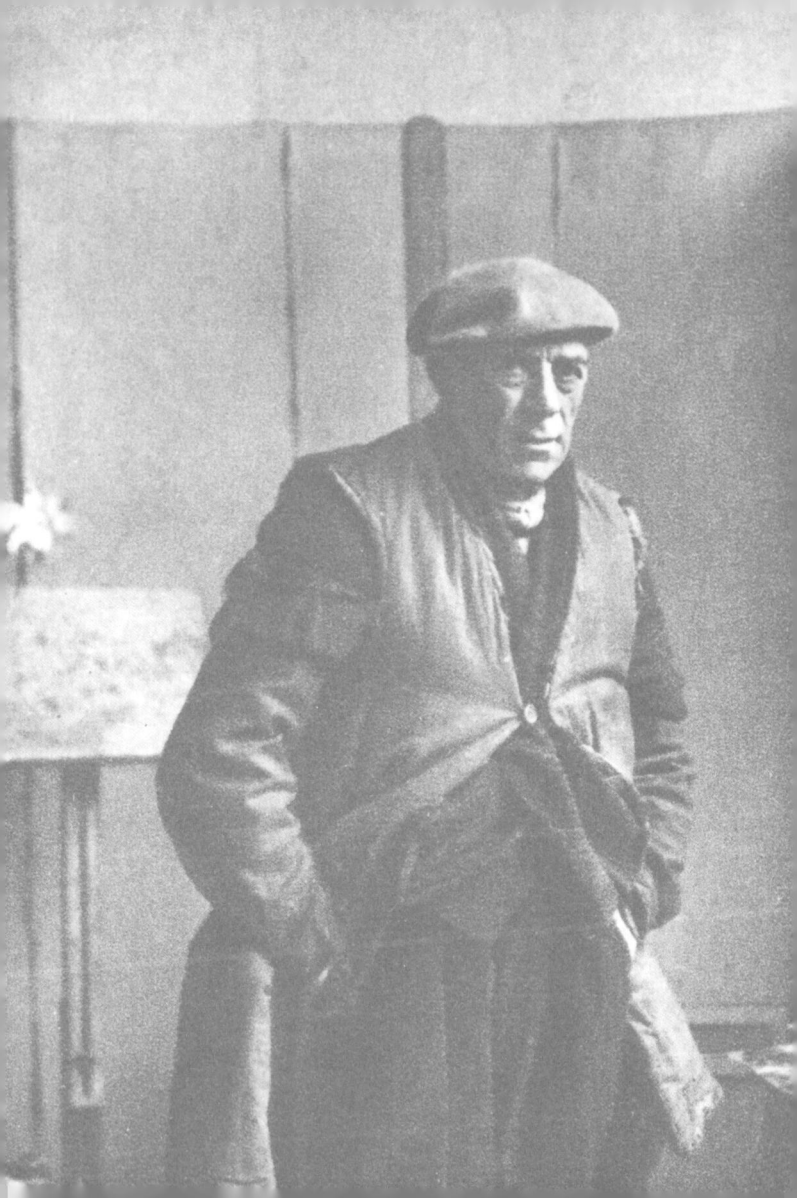

GEORGES BRAQUE

1882–1963

Place of birth/death:

Argenteuil, France/Paris, France

Key works:

Houses at l'Estaque (1908)
Bottle and Fishes (1910–12)
Violin and Candlestick (1910)
Fruit Dish on a Checkered Tablecloth (1917)

EARLY YEARS

Georges Braque was born in the north of France and grew up in the port of Le Havre. He trained to be a painter and decorator to follow in his father's footsteps, but he also studied to be an artist and showed promise. By 1902 he had moved to Paris and was studying painting at the Académie Humbert.

GEORGES BRAQUE

INFLUENCE AND STYLE

Braque's early work was in the style of the
Impressionists, who were still popular
at the turn of the century. But he was
impressed by the bold, colourful work of
Fauvist (wild beasts) painters, including
André Derain and Henri Matisse.

In 1907 the Paul Cézanne memorial
exhibition in Paris was a significant
influence on him, encouraging a change in
style that was to become Cubism.

"Progress in art does not consist in reducing limitations, but in knowing them better."

GEORGES BRAQUE,
GEORGES BRAQUE BY KAREN WILKIN, 1991

CUBIST PIECES

Not long afterwards, Braque met
the Spanish artist Pablo Picasso.
They painted together and soon
became the core artists of the
Cubist movement.

Between 1908 and 1912, Braque
painted many classic Cubist pieces,
including *Houses at L'Estaque* and *Five
Bananas and Two Pears* (both 1908).

SAME BUT DIFFERENT

It is almost impossible to distinguish between many of the works of Braque and Picasso that were painted when they were together around 1911. Picasso's *Still Life with a Violin* and Braque's *Violin and Palette* (both 1911) are of exactly the same subject, and it is likely that the two sat together during the painting sessions.

YOUNG TALENT

Braque worked closely with Picasso
and the two of them began to
incorporate collage in their paintings.
In 1914 Braque joined the army
and was seriously injured in 1915 in
Carency. He suffered from temporary
blindness as a result and did not fully
recover for a few years.

"The only
valid thing
in art is that
which cannot
be explained."

GEORGES BRAQUE,
THE OBSERVER, 1957

BACK AT WORK

Braque was painting again by 1916 but his style had changed. His work became more colourful and more textured, but it still retained the rigid structure he was famous for.

He continued to paint, draw and sculpt for the rest of his life, and work by Braque can be found in museums and art galleries all around the world.

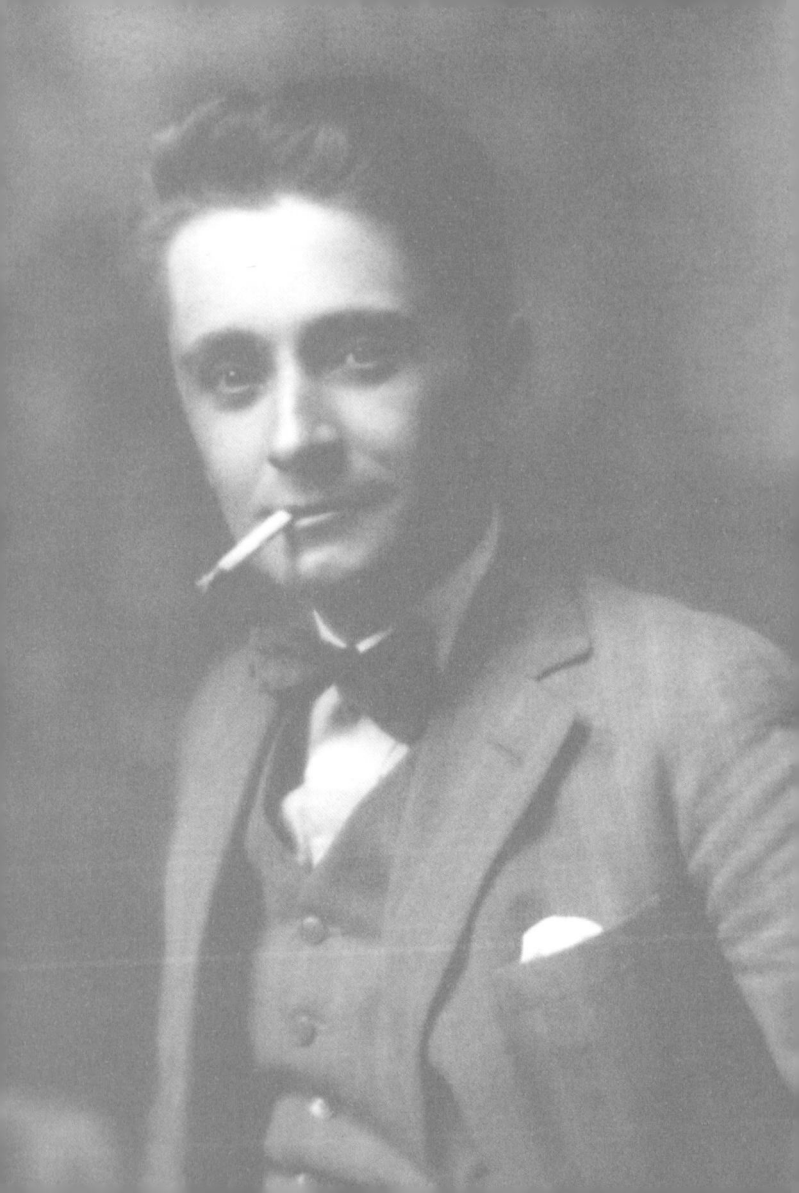

JEAN METZINGER

1883–1956

Place of birth/death:

Nantes, France/Paris, France

Key works:

Bathers: Two Nudes in an Exotic Landscape
(c. 1905)
La danse, Baccante (c. 1906)
Two Nudes (1910–11)
At the Cycle-Race Track (1912)
Woman with a Horse (1911–12)

EARLY YEARS

Jean Dominique Antony Metzinger was born in Nantes, in the west of France, in 1883. His background was a strong military one, with decorated soldiers going back generations in his family. However, his mother was a music professor, and it was likely that she influenced him to turn to the arts.

In 1900 he enrolled at the Académie Cours Cambronne in Nantes to formally study painting.

STYLE

As with other Cubist artists, Cézanne was a significant influence on Metzinger. His earliest paintings were also influenced by the Post-Impressionist Henri-Edmond Cross and Neo-Impressionist Georges Seurat, both of whom worked extensively with landscape and colour.

In addition to his extensive work as a Cubist artist, Metzinger overlapped with the artistic movements of Fauvism, Pointillism and Surrealism.

WORKING ARTIST

Metzinger was successful as an artist almost immediately. In 1908 he took part in an exhibition at Wilhelm Uhde's gallery in Paris that also featured work by Georges Braque and Pablo Picasso.

Very early in his career Metzinger worked with the faceting of form, one of the defining characteristics of Cubism, so he was part of the avant-garde Parisian art scene at the time.

Metzinger incorporated mathematics into his art more overtly than other Cubists, with an emphasis on strict geometric shapes and mathematical proportions.

"My conviction
was justified:
art, that which
lasts, is based on
mathematics."

JEAN METZINGER,
CUBISM WAS BORN, 1972

ART AND EXHIBITION

In 1906 Metzinger met Albert
Gleizes and the two became great
friends, sharing a love of painting
and discussion of theory and
practice, and of how it relates to
mathematics and perspective.

They wrote extensively on various
subjects. Most significantly, they
co-wrote *"Cubism"* in 1912.

TWO NUDES

BY JEAN METZINGER, 1910–11

Location: Gothenburg Museum of Art, Sweden

This painting was part of the first Cubism exhibition in Paris, in 1911. It portrays two figures in what was referred to as Metzinger's "mobile perspective", which examined an object from different angles at the same time. Coupled with masterful use of colour and shading, *Two Nudes* has an almost magical effect on the viewer.

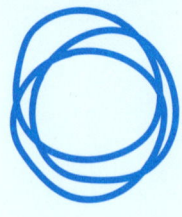

WRITING

Another of Metzinger's written works, *Notes on Painting*, 1910, discusses at length the notion of moving around an object to view (and paint) it from different viewpoints. This notion of time, with repeated viewing of a subject, was especially significant in Cubism.

Some of Metzinger's early works seem to be made up of geometric patterns of colour, serving to highlight the evolution of the artist as a visual communicator.

"Art belongs to the domain of the unreal and it is only when people try to make a reality of it that it falls apart."

JEAN METZINGER,
CUBISM WAS BORN, 1972

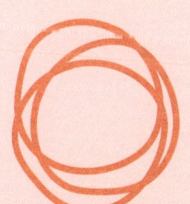

LATER YEARS

After the First World War, Metzinger continued to paint in his own way, moving away from strict Cubism to a more figurative style, incorporating elements of realism. He exhibited frequently and worked until his death in 1956.

Metzinger's most expensive auction sales were *Landscape* (*c.* 1916–17), which sold for $2.3m in 2007, and *The Cyclist* (1912), which realized $3.9m in 2020.

"Instead of copying Nature, we [Cubists] create a 'milieu', of our own, wherein our sentiment can work itself out through a juxtaposition of colours."

JEAN METZINGER,
THE ARCHITECTURAL REVIEW, 1910

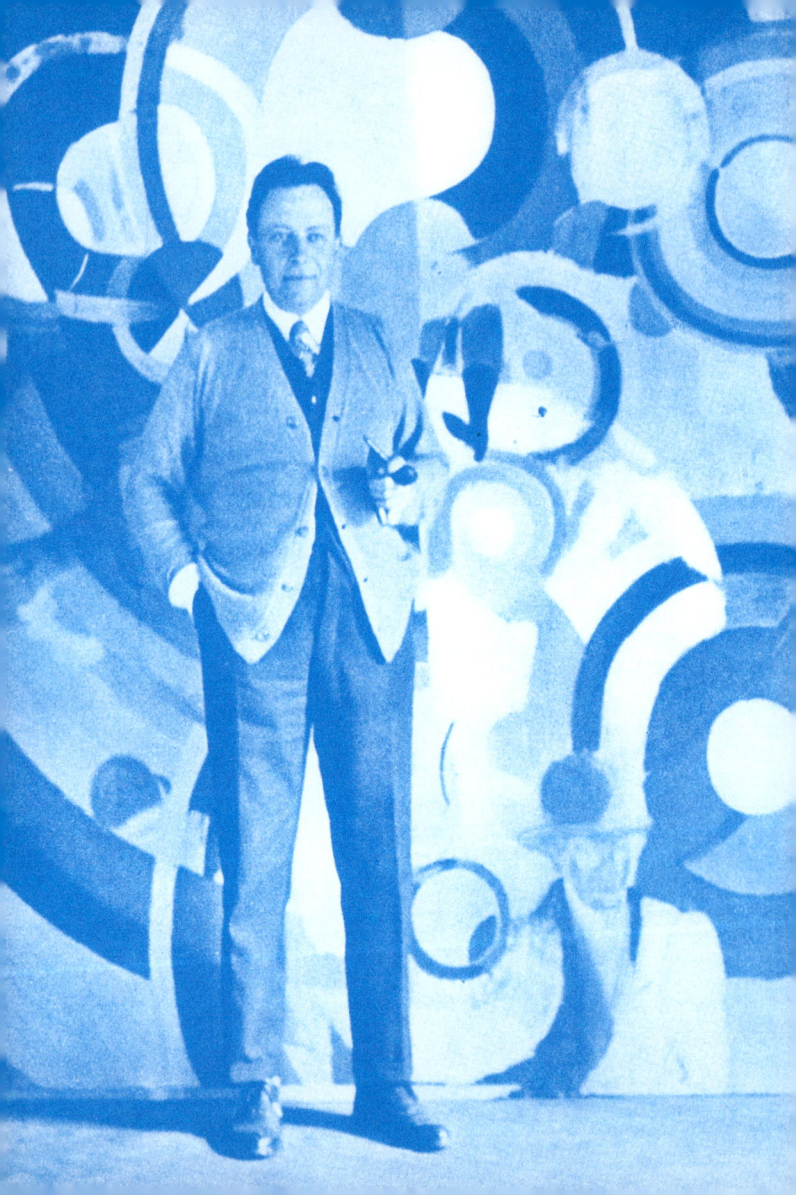

ROBERT DELAUNAY

1885–1941

Place of birth/death:

Paris, France/Montpellier, France

Key works:

*L'Homme à la tulipe (Portrait de
Jean Metzinger)* (1906)
Red Eiffel Tower (1911–12)
The Cardiff Team (1912–13)
Simultaneous Windows (2nd Motif, 1st Part) (1912)

EARLY YEARS

Robert Delaunay was born in 1885 in Paris to an upper-class family. After he finished school, he initially trained in decorative arts and theatre design but soon shifted to painting.

By his early twenties, he was already experimenting with abstract imagery, light and motion in his paintings.

TO PARIS, FRANCE

Delaunay was influenced by Neo-Impressionism and colour theory and he developed a distinctive style. He is known for his use of vibrant colour, dynamic composition and abstraction.

Contrary to the muted tones of early Cubism, Delaunay embraced bold hues and circular forms. His work often evokes movement, light and energy in an urban setting.

In the early 1910s, he co-founded Orphism, a style which mixed the structure of Cubism with the colour work favoured by Fauvist painters.

"As long as art cannot get free from the object, it will continue to be a description."

ROBERT DELAUNAY,
PAUL KLEE BY SUSANNA PARTSCH, 2003

SIMULTANEOUS WINDOWS (2ND MOTIF, 1ST PART)

BY ROBERT DELAUNAY, 1912

Location: Hamburger Kunsthalle, Hamburg, Germany

This painting shows Delaunay's use of colour and fragmented form to depict urban energy. The overlapping windows evoke shifting perspectives, and it is filled with vibrant hues. Unlike Cubism's usual austerity, the painting radiates movement and light. It is a joyful, abstract celebration of modern life.

EVOLUTION

Delaunay's art evolved from its early Cubist influences into a more abstract style. His famous painting series of "windows" and "discs" from 1912–13 reflect this shift.

In the years following the First World War, he explored theatrical set design and large murals, maintaining his core interest in dynamic colour and visual harmony.

"I made paintings that seemed like prisms compared to the Cubism my fellow artists were producing. I was the heretic of Cubism."

ROBERT DELAUNAY,
*THE NEW ART OF COLOR: THE WRITINGS OF
ROBERT AND SONIA DELAUNAY*, 1978

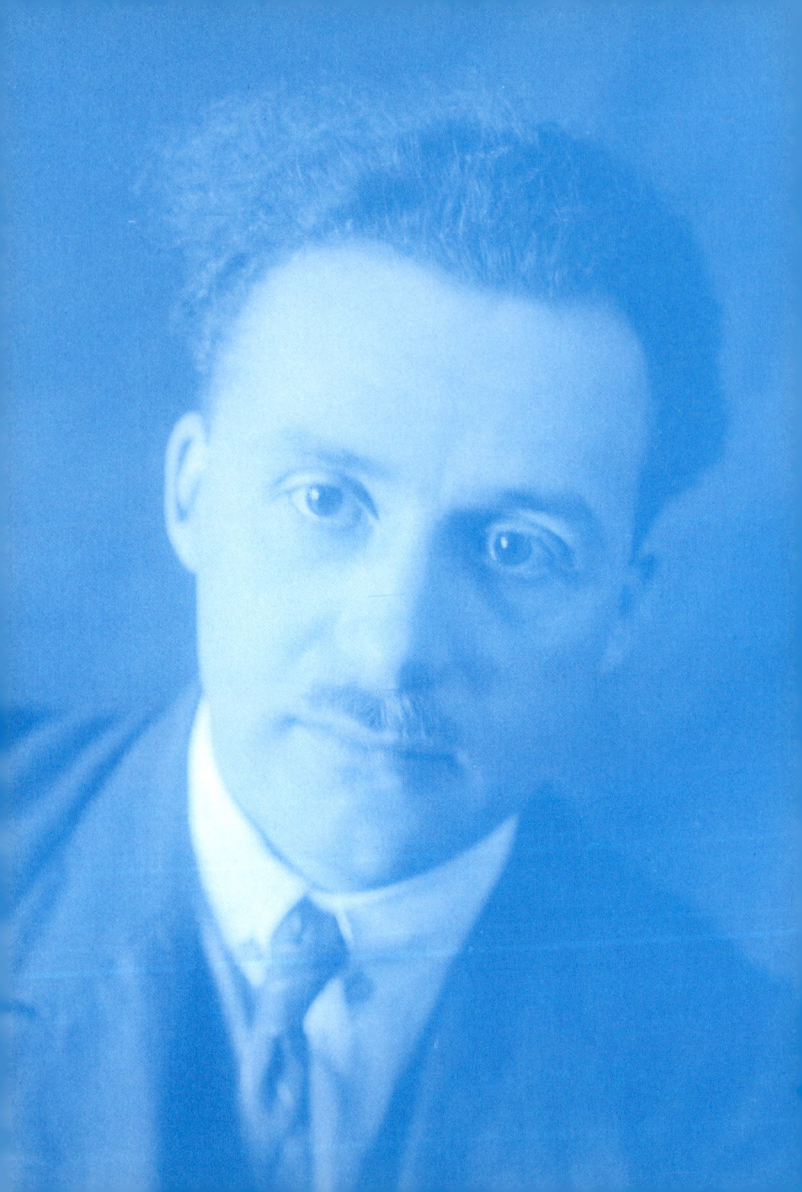

ANDRÉ LHOTE

1885–1962

Place of birth/death:

Bordeaux, France/Paris, France

Key works:

The Great Forest (1908)
La Bacchante ou Nu allongé dans un paysage (1911)
Port of Bordeaux (1911)
The Stopover (1913)
Rugby (1917)

EARLY YEARS

André Lhote was born in Bordeaux, France in 1885. He became an apprentice to a local furniture maker, where he learned to work with wood. By 1904 he was studying decorative sculpture in the École des Beaux-Arts in Bordeaux.

In 1906 he moved to Paris to join the art scene there, and he was part of the founding group of Cubists that emerged shortly afterwards.

EVOLUTION AND STYLE

As with other Cubist artists, Lhote's style was originally closer to Fauvism, with its bright colours and wild brushwork. However, he soon settled into a style closer to the Cubism of Picasso and Braque.

Lhote exhibited his painting *Port of Bordeaux* at the 1911 Salon d'Automne in Paris, alongside works by Gleizes and Metzinger.

"At the end of
the working day,
painters, those great
talkers, go to cafés
where they meet
other painters."

ANDRÉ LHOTE
LA PEINTURE LIBÉRÉE, 1956

WARTIME BREAK

The First World War caused Lhote to pause his artistic career while he fought in the army until 1917.

After the war he resumed his painting, and he was taken on as a client by the prominent dealer Léonce Rosenberg. Lhote also began to teach art at the Académie Notre-Dame des Champs and started writing for the artistic periodical *La nouvelle revue française*.

PORT OF BORDEAUX

BY ANDRÉ LHOTE, 1911

Location: Private collection

Lhote painted the subject matter of his hometown many times, and his style seems to change with each version. In this painting the vibrant maritime scene has a distinct Cubist structure. The bustling port is painted in geometric forms and a flattened perspective, and Lhote's use of colour and recognizable forms make the work feel both modern and accessible.

"It's exciting to capture a moving spectacle where everything seems to stand still for a second before starting up again at an even faster rate."

ANDRÉ LHOTE,
CHRISTIES.COM, 2023

"All I know about photography I learned from André Lhote. There must be freedom, yes, but always with a sense of form and structure behind it."

HENRI CARTIER-BRESSON,
THE NEW YORK TIMES, 2023

LATER YEARS

Lhote taught at the Académie
de Notre-Dame des Champs
until 1922 and then at the school
he founded in Paris, the Academy
André Lhote. His students included
Henri Cartier-Bresson, Simon
Elwes and Shirley Russell.

Lhote travelled extensively and
lectured around the world
until his death in 1962.

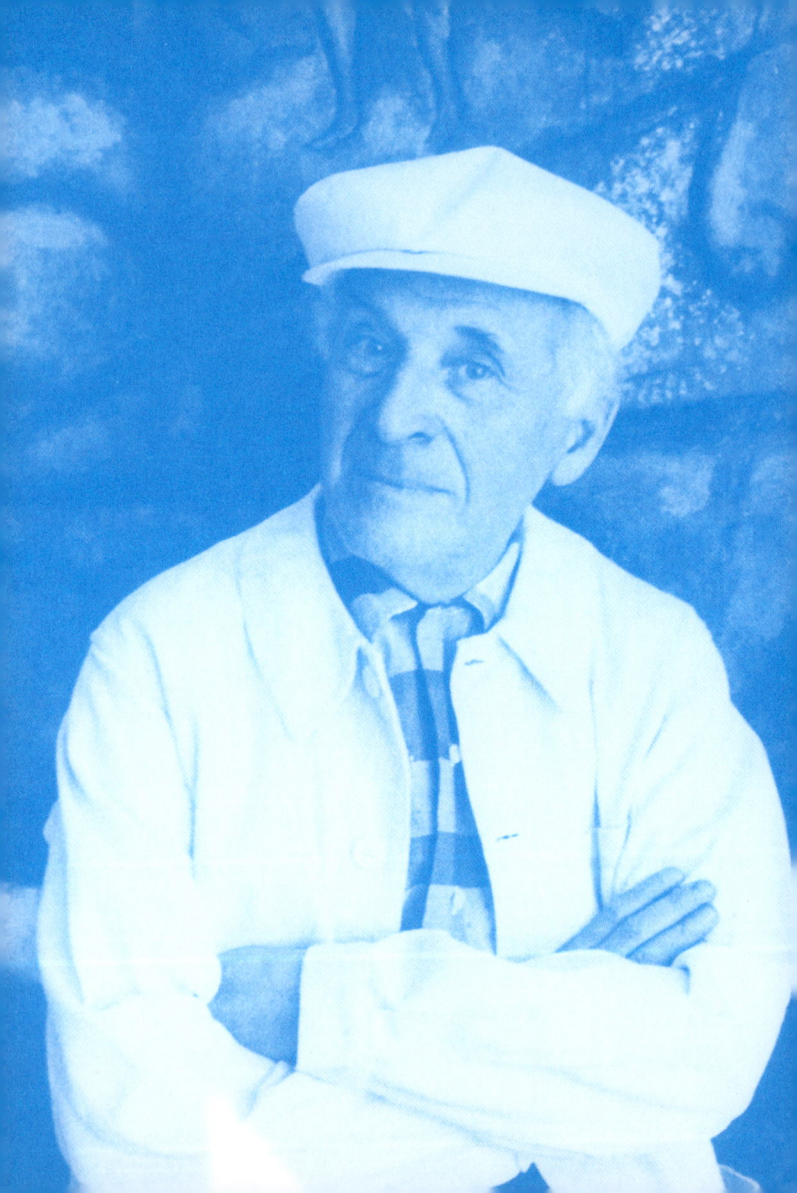

MARC CHAGALL

1887–1985

Place of birth/death:

Liozna, Russian Empire (now Belarus)/
Saint-Paul-de-Vence, France

Key works:

I and the Village (1911)
Paris Through the Window (1913)
Bella with White Collar (1917)
Green Violinist (1923–24)
Peace Window (1967)

EARLY YEARS

Marc Chagall was born Moishe Shagal in 1887 during the Russian Empire. He was the oldest of nine children. From 1907 he studied in Saint Petersburg, at the Imperial Society for the Protection of the Arts, and then with painter Léon Bakst.

In 1910 he moved to Paris, where he encountered the dominant art forms of the time: Fauvism and Cubism. Unable to speak French, Chagall learned quickly and immersed himself in the artistic centres of the city, mixing with other artists.

"I don't know where he [Chagall] gets those images; he must have an angel in his head."

PABLO PICASSO,
MARC CHAGALL – A BIOGRAPHY
BY SIDNEY ALEXANDER, 1978

I AND THE VILLAGE

BY MARC CHAGALL, 1911

Location: Museum of Modern Art, New York, USA

This painting blends dream-like imagery with Cubist structure. There are fragmented forms, overlapping planes and shifting perspectives in Cubist style, and the painting is also playful and personal. The folkloric subject matter contrasts with the analytical approach of Cubism, in a mixture of abstraction, memory and personal symbolism.

MOVING AROUND

Chagall visited Russia in 1914 and was prevented from returning to Paris by the outbreak of the First World War. He settled in Vitebsk, where he was appointed Commissar for Art in 1918 and founded the Vitebsk Popular Art School.

Later he moved to Moscow, where he made stage designs for the State Jewish Chamber Theatre.

In 1923 he returned to Paris to live and work, and he was based there until the Second World War.

WAR AND BEYOND

In 1941 Chagall went to live in the USA to seek refuge from the Nazis. After the war, in 1946, the Museum of Modern Art in New York staged a retrospective of his work.

Chagall settled permanently in France in 1948 and subsequently exhibited regularly around Europe. In 1951 he visited Israel and made his first sculptures. During the 1960s, Chagall worked on many large-scale commissions.

LONG CAREER

Chagall's style changed throughout his life and his work is varied, although there are many recurring themes, including love, faith and the human condition.

Chagall is particularly well-known for his later public works: he designed a ceiling for the Paris Opéra (1964); a window for the United Nations building, New York (1964); murals for the Metropolitan Opera House, New York (1967); and windows for the cathedral in Metz, France (1968). He died in 1968.

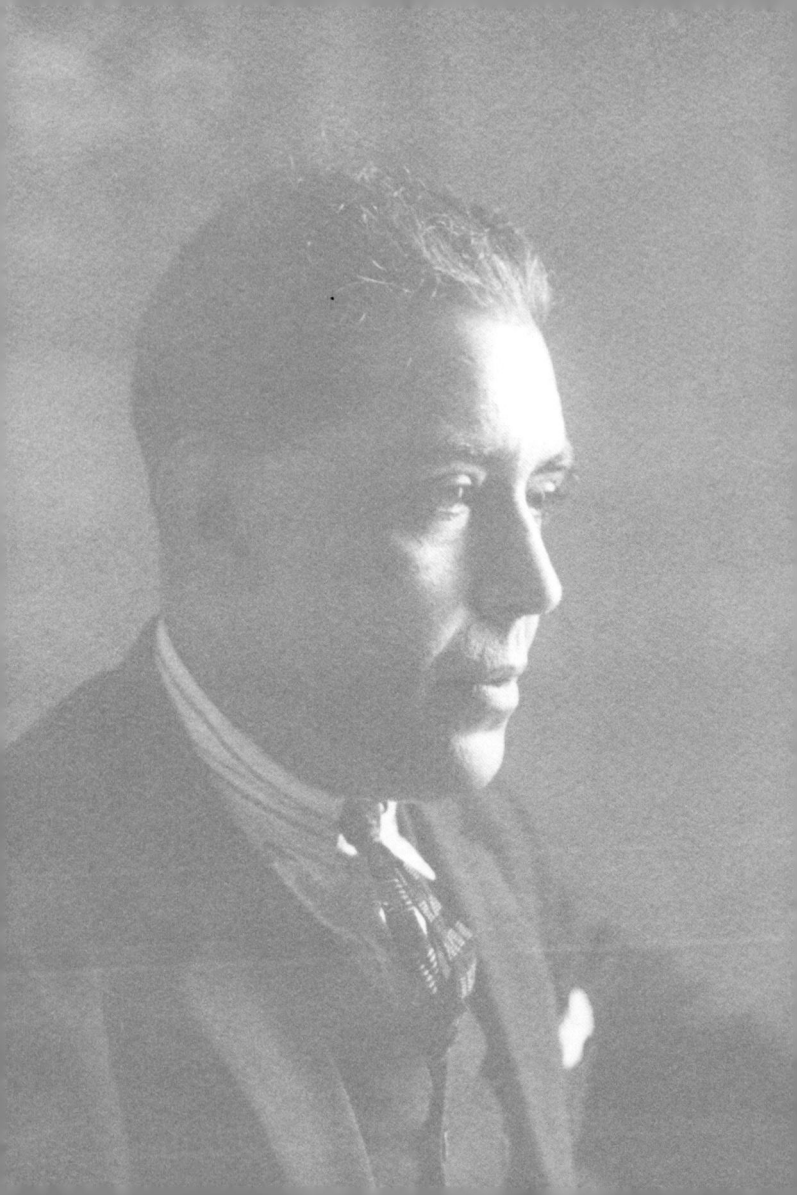

JUAN GRIS

1887–1927

Place of birth/death:

Madrid, Spain/Paris, France

Key works:

Portrait of Picasso (1912)
Man in the Cafe (1912)
Violin and Glass (1915)
Still Life with Checked Tablecloth (1915)
Harlequin with a Guitar (1918)

EARLY YEARS

José Victoriano González-Pérez, known as Juan Gris, was born in Madrid in Spain in 1887. He attended the Madrid School of Arts and Sciences and, as a young man, some of his drawings were featured in local publications.

In 1904 he started to learn to paint under the tútelage of Spanish artist José Maria Carbonero. By 1906 he decided to move to Paris, the centre of the European arts scene.

"No work which is destined to become a classic can look like the classics which have preceded it."

JUAN GRIS,
THE TRANSATLANTIC REVIEW, 1925

CAREER CHANGE

Gris established himself in Paris, mixing with Guillaume Apollinaire, Henri Matisse and the Cubist artists Georges Braque, Fernand Léger and Jean Metzinger.

Until 1911 he worked as a satirical cartoonist, but then he concentrated full-time on his own painting.

Gris was heavily influenced by the painting *Tea Time* (1911) by Jean Metzinger, which introduced Gris to the concept of mathematics in painting.

PORTRAIT OF PICASSO

BY JUAN GRIS, 1912

Location: Art Institute of Chicago, Illinois, USA

This painting clearly demonstrates the principles of Analytical Cubism, with its fragmented planes, subdued colour palette and layered perspective. It honours Picasso while applying Cubist principles to the subject himself, in a work that succeeds in merging both form and identity.

MODERN LIFE

By 1912 Gris was a successful painter, and his work was exhibited around Europe, including at the first declared group Cubist exhibition, the Exposició d'Art Cubista in Barcelona. Such was the painting talent of Gris that Gertrude Stein wrote in *The Autobiography of Alice B. Toklas* he was "the only person whom Picasso wished away".

It was Gris who coined the term "Analytical Cubism" to describe his work, and he painted with vibrant colours, unlike Braque and Picasso at the time.

"Cubism is not a manner but an aesthetic, and even a state of mind."

JUAN GRIS,
JUAN GRIS, HIS LIFE AND WORK
BY DANIEL-HENRY KAHNWEILER, 1947

"I always pet a dog with my left hand, because if he bit me, I'd still have my right hand to paint with."

JUAN GRIS,
*WASHBOAT DAYS: MONTMARTRE, PICASSO
AND THE ARTISTS' REVOLUTION*
BY JANINE WARNOD, 1972

EVOLUTION

Gris embraced Synthetic Cubism and from 1916 onwards his style changed. It evolved to become simpler in structure and feature overlapping shapes and colours, often causing a blend of a painting's subject and its background. He continued to use strong colours.

In 1924, Gris worked on costumes and set design for the Ballets Russes in Paris.

LATER YEARS

Gris died from kidney failure in 1925, at the young age of 40 years old. He had painted around 215 artworks, although some sources list as many as 270 in total. The vast majority of his works are still lifes.

His 1915 painting *Still Life with Checked Tablecloth* was sold in 2014 for more than $57m at auction, and many of his paintings have sold for tens of millions of dollars.

"I try to make concrete that which is abstract."

JUAN GRIS,
L'ESPRIT NOUVEAU, 1921

"It took me a whole lifetime to paint like a child."

PABLO PICASSO,
PICASSO, MY GRANDFATHER BY MARINA
PICASSO, 2001